To my beautiful family. A.M.

First published in Great Britain 2023 by Red Shed, part of Farshore
An imprint of HarperCollins*Publishers*
1 London Bridge Street, London SE1 9GF
www.farshore.co.uk

HarperCollins*Publishers*
Macken House, 39/40 Mayor Street Upper, Dublin 1 D01 C9W8

Text copyright © Ant Middleton 2023
Ant Middleton has asserted his moral rights.
Illustrations © HarperCollins*Publishers* 2023
Cover photograph © Pål Hansen 2023
Target artwork (throughout) © Shutterstock 2023

Consultancy by Dr Miquela Walsh, DEdPsych, MsC (Dist), BSc (Hons), HCPC accredited.

ISBN 978 0 7555 0380 3
Printed and bound in Bosnia and Herzegovina by GPS Group.
001

A CIP catalogue record for this title is available from the British Library.

Stay safe online. Any website addresses listed in this book are correct at the time of going to print.
However, Farshore is not responsible for content hosted by third parties. Please be aware that online
content can be subject to change and websites can contain content that is unsuitable for children.
We advise that all children are supervised when using the internet.

Farshore takes its responsibility to the planet and its inhabitants very seriously.
We aim to use papers from well-managed forests run by responsible suppliers.

MISSION TOTAL CONFIDENCE

ANT MIDDLETON

RED SHED

CONTENTS

Hey there, Ant Middleton reporting for duty! I'm a soldier, adventurer, author, presenter and businessperson. My life has taken me to some of the most amazing and dangerous parts of the planet.

But it's also had its fair share of ups and downs. I lost my dad when I was really young – something I found REALLY hard. And just when I was beginning to feel that things couldn't get any harder . . . my whole family moved to a tiny village in Normandy, France. Suddenly I wasn't just having to cope with my dad's death. I was trying to work out how to cope with a new language and a new school and an environment that felt bewilderingly different from the one I had left behind.

And yet I managed to find my feet. After a while, I began to thrive. By the time I was a teenager, I knew that I wanted to see as much of the world as I possibly could. I was ready for ADVENTURE, which I couldn't really get in the sleepy French countryside. That's why, at the age of seventeen, I joined the British Army. That too was a MASSIVE culture shock. I had to grow up really fast. Sometimes that was frightening, sometimes it was exciting, but it was always interesting, and I learned an incredible amount.

I left the Army after a few years because I realised that I was in the wrong part of it. That gave me the opportunity to go out into the world and try a couple of different careers. I made about ten million mistakes. I also learned a heck of a lot about myself. One of the things I learned was that I still really wanted to be a soldier, so I joined the Royal Marines.

While I was a Royal Marine, I went to fight in Afghanistan. Then I put myself forward for selection into the Specialist Military Unit, which is one of the most elite organisations in the British Armed Forces. In the Specialist Military Unit I went on more missions than I've had hot dinners (which is A LOT); I tested myself in super-extreme weather conditions and came out the other side (just); and I pushed my body and mind further than I ever thought possible (ouch)! These days, you might find me leaping about on your TV screens, a change of career so unexpected that I sometimes wonder whether it's actually a dream.

And do you know what has allowed me to do all of this? The rocket fuel that has allowed me to do amazing things and visit extraordinary places? My muscles? Well, they were useful, but try again. My ability to stay awake for three days straight? Well, that had its place, but I think I could have got by without it. My beard? No! No! No! It's confidence!

By confidence, I'm not talking about being boastful or arrogant. One thing I've learned over the years is that anybody who is always going around telling you how brilliant they are probably doesn't even believe it themselves! **Confidence, for me, is about being comfortable with who I am. It's about being willing to try anything (even if it makes me feel a bit nervous). And it's about having faith in what I'm capable of.**

Being confident has given me the chance to achieve so many of my wildest dreams. It's also helped me cope when times have got tough. And, do you know what the best thing about it is?

It doesn't matter how big or small you are, or how old or young; it doesn't matter what sort of family you come from; it doesn't matter whether you're good at maths and terrible at art. Nobody is born confident. But . . .

EVERYBODY
CAN BECOME
CONFIDENT.

I was once afraid of my own shadow. Over time I've built up my confidence to the point where I feel as if I can cope with anything life throws at me.

In this book, I'll show you how to build up *your* confidence. I'm here to share with you some of the tools I've used over the years to help boost my self-belief. I'll also show you many cool things you can do with your new confidence. Most importantly, I want to encourage you to see the world as I do: as a place that is full of adventure, excitement and opportunity, which is just waiting for you to dive in.

But I also need something from you. I need you to realise that you're already a brilliant, unique human being. You probably see the world differently from everybody else. You might have different opinions from the people around you. You will definitely have different strengths and challenges. But that difference is the foundation of your incredible potential.

The tools I give you won't change the person you are; they won't give you bigger muscles or make you taller! But they will help you understand how much you're capable of. **Confidence is the key that will unlock your potential.**

BEING
YOU
IS YOUR

SUPERPOWER.

I also want you to know that if you have days when it feels as if these tools aren't working, that's OK! It's not because you're failing at being confident. It's because you're human.

When you're feeling like that, be kind to yourself. Confidence is not about 'doing', 'achieving', 'succeeding' or 'failing'; it is about knowing who you are and celebrating this. If you want some quiet time, go for it – have the confidence to accept that that is what you need! Have a good sleep, get some exercise . . . whatever helps when you're feeling rubbish. Remember, you've got all kinds of experiences waiting for you, you'll learn to do amazing things and pick up new skills. All of this is possible, and I'm going to help you get there.

Your MISSION, if you choose to accept it, is to develop TOTAL CONFIDENCE.

CHAPTER ONE

BE YOUR OWN CHEERLEADER

Total confidence begins with the way you think about yourself. The problem is that human beings are brilliant at noticing the stuff we feel we're bad at, and very often we're terrible at spotting the things that we're good at. When we peer into the mirror, all we can see are the things that we don't like very much. And we don't see any of our strengths. Maybe you're the same?

It probably won't come as a surprise when I tell you that when you do this, it's really hard to build any sort of confidence in yourself. I'm a big believer in being as honest with yourself as you possibly can be. But being honest isn't the same as tearing your personality to pieces. The way I see it, being honest is just as much about identifying and celebrating the things we're good at, as it is about working out those areas where we could perhaps improve.

Let's start by focussing on your achievements. I'm certain that you've got far more to celebrate than you realise. All the stuff you've learned, all the tests you've passed. Perhaps you've worked hard to become totally amazing at jazz dancing or absolutely flipping incredible at Minecraft. Or it could be that you're always the first person to put your hand up in class to volunteer when somebody else needs help.

And think about all of the challenges (big and small) that you've overcome. As I always like to say,

YOU'VE SURVIVED

100 PER CENT

OF YOUR DIFFICULT DAYS.

Perhaps you've started at a new school where you don't know anybody, or stood up in front of an audience to play an instrument, or you've helped defend a friend who was being picked on by a bully?

> Take a moment to consider all of the difficult stuff you've managed to cope with already. Write a list of things you have found challenging but have overcome and things you are good at. Perhaps you made a new friend on a school trip that you'd been nervous about going on. Or maybe you love drawing and can create pictures that make you feel happy.

The second you realise that, actually, you ARE pretty darn good at quite a few things, and that you actually DO have the ability to cope with unfamiliar or challenging situations, it will change the way you feel about yourself. You can become your own cheerleader. (Sparkly outfit and pompoms optional!)

I believe that doing *something* is always better than doing *nothing*. When you're actively trying to provide solutions to problems, it helps you feel more in control of that situation and gives your brain less time and space to get all twisted up with uncomfortable thoughts. That's true when it comes to those one-off events in life that make you anxious (like the prospect of having to go to a new school), but it's also true when it comes to the stuff that feels quite challenging in your everyday life (maybe you find meeting new people hard).

It's also important to remember that 'doing' doesn't have to involve jumping around and being super active. It could just be sitting still for a few seconds and trying to notice what thoughts are swirling round and round in your brain. Don't hide from those feelings or pretend that they're not there. When I can sense anxiety mounting inside me, I turn to face it. 'Oh, hello, feeling of worry, why are you here? Can you leave now, please, I do not need you!'

*Write down three things you love and enjoy doing,
and three challenges you're currently facing. Now,
beside each one, write what you can do to make
the most of those things you love, or what you can
do to overcome those challenges. For example:*

*Something I love: I'm good at badminton. If
I practise more, I might be picked for the team.*

*Something I feel challenged by: I hate the idea
of standing up and speaking in front of large
groups. If I try to give some little presentations
to smaller groups first, I'll gain confidence.*

**Part of establishing a solid foundation of confidence
comes through learning to love and appreciate the person
you are.** It's easier to be a truly confident person if you're
not pretending you're something, or someone, you're not.

Never forget that you are amazing. You're not perfect.
Nobody is. In fact, you're better than that. You're a unique
human being full of different likes and dislikes, which
will probably change and grow as you change and grow
yourself. Don't wish any of it away. It's all an important
part of what makes you, er, you.

Draw a picture of yourself on a piece of paper and then add some thought bubbles with positive things about yourself (use the list you created in the mission on page 19 to help you). For example:

I am loved.
I am brave.
I make people laugh.

Hang it up on your wall and try saying one of the positive statements every day to help you remember why you're special.

Of course, there will be days when you can't help noticing how much you like the way that somebody else talks or acts. Or they might dress in a way that you think is cooler than the way you do. I believe we should all be looking to absorb cool stuff from watching other people. That's how we learn! But why would you want to copy EVERYTHING about that person? Equally, there will be times when you feel tempted to squash yourself into a shape that you think will help you fit in. You worry that if you show the world who you really are, you might be rejected or made fun of.

**But what a waste of time it is to pretend to like
Billie Eilish, when you'd much prefer to listen to Bach!**
And how rubbish it can feel to be so desperate to fit in with
everyone else that you wear the same types of clothes as
your friends, even though you feel much happier wearing
something else! And yet we've all done this, or at the very
least been tempted to. I'm no different.

At the beginning of my time in the Army, I was anxious to
be accepted by a group of people who were older than me.
I copied the way that they spoke and dressed (jumpers with
holes in them, ripped jeans and desert boots, in case you
were wondering) and I went along with them even when they
were doing rowdy, stupid stuff that I knew was wrong. I was
so focused on copying others that I neglected the things
that I was good at and were important to me. I suppressed
the sensitive, empathetic side of my personality and forced
myself to pretend that I was interested in doing stuff that
I flipping hated. I wanted to improve myself by learning new
skills or going to the gym; they just wanted to go out and
get into fights. But because I also really wanted to fit in,
I agreed to join in with the things they wanted to do.

Somewhere along the line, I lost confidence in who I was
and where I wanted to be heading. My own sense of my
value was entirely dependent on what the other lads in
my regiment thought or said about me. You probably don't
need me to tell you that this was a **TERRIBLE** idea.

NO MATTER HOW HARD YOU TRY...

YOU'RE NEVER GOING TO BE ABLE TO CONTROL WHAT OTHER PEOPLE THINK ABOUT YOU!

They're always going to reach their own conclusions.
So why even try? If someone else doesn't like or appreciate
you as you actually are, then they're probably not someone
that you should be looking to hang out with.

It's far better to focus on being happy with the person YOU already are. Don't worry about what ANYBODY ELSE thinks! If listening to rock music gives you joy, then great! If reading science fiction makes you happy, GO FOR IT!

If you find yourself in a similar situation to the one I just described, stop and ask yourself, are you doing this to . . .

- Impress someone?
- Because you're worried people might laugh at you?
- Because everyone else is?

Are these the right reasons?

I promise you that the most important thing of all isn't whether other people like you; it's that you like yourself.

The people around you, like your friends and family, don't need or want you to be anybody other than who you are. They're never going to say, 'Oh, I'll like you when you become a lawyer or a celebrity chef,' or 'I'll like you if you start listening to COOL music.' They ALREADY think the person you are RIGHT NOW is amazing.

YOU'RE THE BEST IN THE WORLD AT BEING YOU.

WHY ON EARTH WOULD
YOU WANT TO BE ANYONE ELSE?

DIFFICULT DAYS

It's important to acknowledge that we all have days when things feel as if they're going really well and days when everything seems to go wrong. There will be times you're so blimmin' full of confidence that you'll believe you're capable of anything. And you may also have moments when you barely feel capable of getting to the end of your road. Or when you look around thinking that everybody else is better than you and that you don't belong.

That's OK. If you're having a difficult day, try to remind yourself that that's all it is. It won't last for ever. Tomorrow you'll probably feel different.

If you're feeling sad a lot of the time, have low energy levels and low confidence, then know that you're not alone and that lots of people are there to help you. The strongest thing to do is to ask for help. **Talk to a family member, friend or trusted adult.**

Remember those statements you made earlier for your mission on page 22? Keep reminding yourself that being YOU is a superpower, one that you've already used to overcome all sorts of challenges! You are stronger than you think.

CHAPTER TWO
BRICK BY BRICK

People try to build their confidence in all sorts of ways. They employ hypnotists to convince them that they can take on the world. They stare at themselves in the mirror and say to themselves, 'I am a TIGER!' and then they'll let loose a big full-throated grrrrrooooowwwwll and hope nobody else was listening. I also heard of one man who paid somebody to whisper 'You are brilliant' into his ear over and over again.

My approach is much more straightforward. There aren't any gurus or magic tricks, and you don't have to pretend to be the king of the jungle. You just have to be willing to put in a little bit of effort. At the end of the day, you've got to do what works for YOU.

When I was a bit younger (OK, a LOT younger) and just getting to grips with life in France, one thing that was pretty scary was trying to speak AN ENTIRELY NEW language. We'd done a bit of practice, but, well, nothing prepares you for how stupidly difficult it is to follow what a French kid is saying to you when he seems to be speaking at approximately ten million miles an hour.

The first time I tried to say anything in French, it went terribly. The words came out in a rush, and I stumbled. The whole class laughed at me. If there had been some way of escaping to Mars and never coming back, you better believe I'd have jumped right on that spaceship.

And it wasn't just that. Pretty soon I realised that the fact that I couldn't speak the language very well also meant that every single class I took was a struggle. When I'd open up the exercise book I'd stare and stare, hoping that the jumble of French words in front of me would suddenly start making sense. It felt like I was living through a nightmare!

Slowly – very slowly – I started picking up the language, and after a while, I'd learned enough to get by (I'll talk about how I managed this in a bit more detail later). And yet at the same time, all the other kids in my class seemed to be doing so much better than me. It was easy for them, I told myself, they already spoke French perfectly! I began to feel quite down; I didn't want to go to school, and I found it hard to motivate myself.

My view became something like this: What is the point in me even trying if I am never going to be as good as the others? It's NOT FAIR. It felt as if I was about to run a race with the rest of the people in my class. Sometimes I'd take one look at the homework I took home with me and say, 'This is too hard, I'm never going to get it right in a million years. I'm still going to be the worst in the class, so why bother?' Then I'd go outside to play, trying not to think about what would happen when I turned up to school yet again with a book full of unanswered maths questions.

I can't remember what it was that made me see things in a different light. Perhaps I just got tired of sulking all the time, but eventually a moment came when I told myself that there was no use feeling upset and angry because the others all appeared to be sailing through every test. The important thing, I realised, was just to do a bit better than I had the last time round. And I stopped comparing myself to what anybody else was doing – because what they did or did not achieve was COMPLETELY IRRELEVANT to me.

I worked harder than I had before. Most importantly, I didn't give up every time I came across an essay or a maths assignment that appeared to be tricky. Sometimes I got the answers right, sometimes I got the answers wrong, but because I was giving questions a go rather than just throwing my hands up and claiming that they were too hard, I was handing myself a chance.

WHEN I MADE A

MISTEAK

~~MISTAEK~~

~~MISTAYK~~

MISTAKE

I TRIED TO LEARN FROM IT.
I DIDN'T SUDDENLY BECOME

A GENIUS

– OF COURSE I DIDN'T!

Still, every time we took a test, or handed in a project, I did a little bit better. I didn't feel daunted when I was asked a question in class. And instead of dreading school, I started to look forward to it.

What had felt like the MOST UNFAIR THING IN HISTORY (being sent to a French school) actually turned out to be one of the best things that could have happened to my confidence. Sometimes where we are right now is EXACTLY where we need to be. I had been given the chance to slowly build my self-belief. I realised that if I was capable of learning a new language while simultaneously settling into a new school, I was probably capable of a load of other things too. I had felt intimidated by what seemed like an impossible challenge, but what I'd learned was that no situation lasts for ever – we always have the capacity to change and grow.

I started using this approach everywhere else in my life. The more I demonstrated to myself that I was able to learn how to improve at *specific* stuff, the more my *general* confidence grew. I began to really trust myself and my abilities. That meant I was much more willing to try new things, even when I found them a bit frightening to begin with. And on those occasions when I hit a bump in the road, I knew that I'd be able to cope.

You don't build your confidence by taking great leaps. There aren't any short cuts or life hacks that can help.

We proceed brick by brick, slowly creating a solid foundation of confidence.

Once you have a solid foundation of confidence, you can carry on building and building and building on it. And you'll always be able to go back to it when you need reassuring after you have a difficult day or a setback (and we all do from time to time). Because you know that **your confidence isn't based on what others say or think about you, or the results you get on one test, but on what YOU have shown yourself you're capable of.**

THAT CRUCIAL FIRST STEP

Sometimes, we miss out on exciting opportunities, or don't give ourselves the chance to learn a brilliant new skill, because we're unwilling to make the first step that will send us on our way.

But one commitment is all it takes to get started. When you're contemplating trying something new, don't feel as if you have to take a massive bite out of the problem, or let yourself get bogged down in thinking about every single thing you might potentially have to deal with at some point. If you do, you'll probably start feeling overwhelmed. It will begin to seem impossible and you'll never want to even try.

I'm actually pretty afraid of enclosed spaces. Even getting into a lift is enough to make me feel nervous. The idea of the lift breaking down and leaving me trapped makes me really anxious. But I am able to get in (even if I don't like it). I once met someone who was so terrified of lifts that they couldn't even put a foot in without having something close to a panic attack. All I asked them to do was to step into a lift and let the doors close behind them for ten seconds, before coming out. That's the only thing they had to do. Ten seconds! In the moments beforehand, they were almost shaking with nerves, **BUT THEY DID IT!** They came out so excited that they were talking at a million miles an hour. It was as if they couldn't believe what had happened. A minute before, they had thought that they were too frightened to ever get into a lift. Now they'd shown themselves that they could stay inside one for ten seconds. It might seem small to you, but to them it was HUGE. Next they stayed in for 30 seconds. And after that they went up one floor. All of that began with one commitment.

It's amazing what you can gain by just committing once, for a few seconds. You start there and who knows where that might lead to. The voice in your head that whispers 'I can't do this, I can't do this' gets transformed into one that is shouting **'I CAN DO IT! I CAN DO IT!'**

Make a list of five new things you'd like to try. Next, write down what first commitment you could make to begin. It can be really small, but remember, every step forward counts!

So, for instance, you might be interested in helping to fight climate change and have discovered that that local activists hold meetings in a venue close to your house. BUT, the idea of standing up and sharing your thoughts and ideas in front of loads of grown-ups and strangers sends a chill down your spine. Your first commitment could be going to one meeting. Next time, maybe you could put your hand up and ask a question. These are all tiny steps. Tiny commitments. But they add up. And who knows where this will lead you?

Never be afraid of making mistakes. It's only by trying and failing, then trying and failing again, that you give yourself the chance to learn and grow. Failure is the best teacher. Remember, you're not aiming for perfection (IT DOESN'T EXIST!). You just want to be making a bit of progress.

When you have a setback, whatever it is you're doing, there's no need to be disheartened or feel as if it's a knock against your confidence. I used to feel quite down every time I didn't do as well as I'd hoped in a test or I got a school report which kept on saying ANT MUST DO BETTER! But they weren't a statement of who I was deep down; they were just measures of how I'd performed in one test on one given day or in one particular class. So, if you've dropped a catch in a big cricket game, it doesn't mean you're rubbish at cricket, it just means that you made one mistake . . . and EVERYONE makes mistakes. Turn on the telly and you'll see professional cricketers – people who have trained for years and years and years until they are the best in the world at what they do – making exactly the same sorts of mistakes as you.

It's OK to feel disappointed and sad when these things happen, but you also need to realise that you've been handed an opportunity to learn. And you can use that disappointment

and sadness to push you to practise and practise
your catching so that you will increase your confidence
in that skill, and reduce your chances of fumbling the
ball next time.

The older I get, the more I have come to understand that

FAILURE ISN'T SOMETHING TO BE *AVOIDED* OR FEARED.

It's something to seek out and celebrate. Because **if you're
putting yourself in a position to fail, you're also putting
yourself in a position to grow**. If you don't take the chance
that you MIGHT drop the ball while trying to catch it, you're
also making sure you'll never experience the excitement of
winning a game, or being part of a team, or slowly, steadily,
mastering a new skill.

There's another thing that embracing the positive aspects
of failure has taught me. I now try to avoid spending so
much time thinking about my destination that I forget to
enjoy the journey. What I mean by this is that it's very easy
to get so obsessed with thinking about how great it will
be when you've FINALLY become an absolutely brilliant
ballerina, that you don't take the opportunity to appreciate

everything you're doing, learning and enjoying RIGHT HERE, RIGHT NOW.

Learning a new skill can be frustrating and tiring, but it can also be fun. You don't need to be Darcey Bussell, you don't need to win any competitions or earn any certificates to realise how amazing it is that you've learned to *glissade*. So remember to pay attention to all those little moments of joy and pride you encounter along the way.

This is something that the famous rugby union player Jonny Wilkinson learned the hard way. His whole life was dedicated to becoming a champion. Day after day, he practised and practised and practised. When he fell short

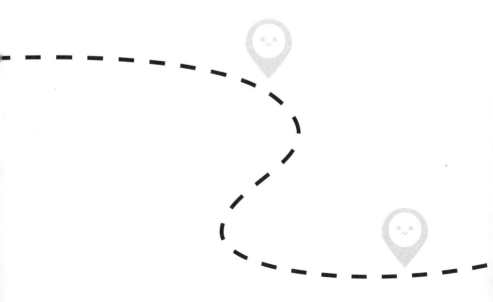

of his phenomenally high standards he was really harsh on himself. Instead of having fun playing a game that he loved, he worried that he was letting people down. Still, he told himself that it would all be worthwhile once he achieved his goal. But, do you know what happened? The morning after he had kicked the goal that won the World Cup for England he woke up feeling terribly sad. He should have been elated, and yet he realised that years had passed and he'd barely looked around him. Loads of stuff had happened and he hadn't really enjoyed it or noticed it because he was so focused on his ambition. Luckily, he has learned since to embrace being in the moment, to take pleasure in what's actually happening in front of him rather than thinking obsessively about a distant point in the future.

THE SUPERHERO'S POSE

Sometimes it's good to give your confidence a little bit of a kickstart, especially on those days when your self-belief appears to be in short supply (and we all have them). The good news is that there are a few things that you can do to help you feel full of positivity. Although they're never going to be a substitute for the slow process of building your internal confidence, they're a brilliant thing to have up your sleeve. You could look at them a bit like the energy drinks you see athletes chucking down their throats. They don't replace all the training those cyclists or runners do, and yet they provide a boost when

It's really needed! Or perhaps think about the costumes a lot of superheroes wear. Putting on a cape doesn't in itself make a superhero any stronger or faster, but it does have a psychological impact.

And you can do something similar! You probably already know that our facial expressions and what we're doing with the rest of our body communicates as much, if not more, to other people as the actual words that come out of our mouths. You can tell as much about what another human being is thinking from looking at their body language as you can from listening to what they say to you. When we're unhappy, our heads droop, we struggle to make eye contact, we might cross our arms. When we're excited, we jump about on the spot, we talk more quickly, there's a big grin on our face. Our bodies are like big signs saying: THIS IS HOW I'M FEELING TODAY.

What's really cool is that you can reverse
this process. Instead of your mind influencing
how your body acts, you can use your body
to influence how your mind feels. Just a few
little changes to your body language can
affect your self-esteem and help you feel
better about yourself. If you ACT as if you're
confident, then you'll start to actually feel as
if you ARE confident.

I know it sounds pretty wild, but there's a
lot of scientific evidence for this connection
between body and mind. For instance, in a
recent experiment it was shown that the
participants who held 'power poses' (see page
45 for what I mean by this!) for a single minute
were more confident about themselves in a job
interview than the participants that didn't do
this exercise. Standing in these attitudes made
them feel stronger and more full of self-belief.
In another study, participants who were told to
sit up straight were more likely to believe that
they were qualified for a particular job than
participants who slouched in their chairs.

Why not give these power poses a go? They'll send a load of confident messages to your brain. They'll also communicate that confidence to anyone you interact with.

1. Keep your chin and head up (a tip for helping with this is to imagine that the top of your head is connected by a string to the ceiling).

2. Stand up straight (put your shoulders back).

3. Stand with your feet in a wide, open stance.

4. Keep your hands out of your pockets.

5. When you're talking to somebody else, smile and maintain eye contact. (If this is something you find difficult, you can try to look at the other person's eyes for two seconds, then their nose for two seconds and then their mouth for two seconds – then repeat. This gives the same effect as looking directly into their eyes.)

We all worry sometimes that our own feelings or likes and dislikes aren't important enough to share with other people. We might even tell ourselves that we should hide them away rather than express them. I know that there have been many occasions in my life when I've been anxious that if I said what I thought, or told people what I wanted, they might react badly. Perhaps there's stuff that sometimes stops you from speaking up and sharing your thoughts? But (and this is really important) . . .

YOUR VOICE DESERVES TO BE HEARD!

And the more you say your thoughts out loud, the more it builds your self-esteem. You're showing everyone around you (including you!) that your thoughts and preferences are worth being expressed to the world.

I understand that it can feel a tiny bit intimidating doing this, especially if you're not used to it, but I thought I'd let you into a secret that might make doing this easier. Just as your body language can alter how people perceive you (and also how you perceive yourself) the way that you express your likes and dislikes, needs and preferences, can make a big difference.

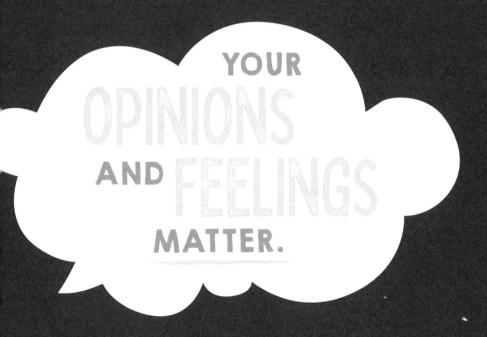

YOUR OPINIONS AND FEELINGS MATTER.

When we're unsure about how our opinions might be received we express them as questions or suggestions. It's almost as though we're keen to show that the idea we've had doesn't really have anything to do with us! So, although we might be absolutely desperate to go to the cinema to watch a film, we end up saying something like . . .

SHALL WE GO AND WATCH A FILM LATER?

(Which is the verbal equivalent of slouching into a room with your eyes focused squarely on the floor.) How about trying something different? Something like . . .

I WOULD LIKE . . . TO GO AND WATCH A FILM LATER.

We call these 'I' statements. They're empowering in the same way that the power poses we talked about earlier in this chapter are.

Other examples include:

I WANT . . .

I THINK . . .

I FEEL . . .

I NEED . . .

MISSION

Start to use more 'I' statements in your everyday life. Perhaps you could begin by practising in front of a mirror? Then you can build up to sharing those opinions with close friends and family. Once you feel comfortable doing that, why not start putting your hand up more in class? What does it feel like to share your opinions and feelings in this way? Does it make you feel confident? Does it change the ways in which other people respond to you?

You could also consider using your voice to help others. If you're in the playground and you see a group of kids being mean to someone, then why not speak up? You could confront the bully yourself, or if you'd prefer, tell an adult. Be a superhero in your own school!

CHAPTER THREE

THINK POSITIVE!

I'm someone who can see the bright side of EVERY situation. Whatever I'm confronted by, I can always find a positive. That means that I'm confident that I'll be able to cope with whatever comes my way. And it makes me much more open to giving things a go when they're outside my comfort zone.

But that's not the same as being somebody who buries their head in the sand and pretends that everything is perfect all of the time. That would be like arguing that the world is flat!

Life can get pretty tricky sometimes. We all have those days when everything is going well and then WHAM! You hit an obstacle. Occasionally those tricky times can stretch out for longer and you start asking yourself: Will it be like this for ever? AAAARGH!

When you're full of confidence, you'll know that although you can be dropped into a situation that looks extremely grim, it's possible to flip it right round so that it starts to look a whole lot better. Because, although you can't stop things that feel bad from happening, you can change the way you think about them.

I realise this might all sound a bit complex, but stay with me, I promise it's much easier than you think.

Whatever is happening to you, whatever you're feeling, one of the best things you can do is to try to identify whatever emotion you're currently dealing with. That's a habit I began when I was still in the military. And I still do it now when I find myself feeling scared or overwhelmed (most often when I have to confront my claustrophobia). These conversations with myself go a bit like this . . .

Q. 'How are you feeling?'

A. 'Well, I'm pretty panicked. Terrified actually.'

Q. 'Why do you think you're feeling so afraid?'

A. 'Well, I'm underground, in quite a dark tunnel, and I really hate enclosed spaces.'

Q. 'What can you do about it?'

A. 'Hmmm, I'm not injured, and there's a guy just ahead of me who knows where the exit is, so I can put my trust in him. I can also start to breathe a bit more slowly and deliberately, which I know helps to make me feel more calm.'

As soon as you can identify an emotion, you can start to grapple with it. Once you're able to grapple with an emotion, you can start to ask yourself how you might make things better. And when your mind turns to thinking up solutions rather than getting swirled up in panic, you will begin to feel calmer.

It's absolutely natural that you'll feel anxious or overwhelmed when you're thinking about something that seems intimidating in the future (such as playing the violin in front of an audience), or something that's actually happening now (you're about to meet a new teacher). Our bodies and minds are trained to react like that – your brain wants to keep you safe. Thanks, brain!

These tricky-feeling situations are EXACTLY the sorts of moments when you need to remind yourself of how much you're capable of (I know, I know, I've already talked about this, but I'll keep going until you acknowledge the thing that I already know: you're stronger than you think).

And what's really exciting is that as well as being able to change the way you think about situations, **you can also change the way you think about yourself!**

All of us are far too quick to forget, or take for granted, the good things in our life. This isn't surprising. We can often be so busy focussing on the stuff that feels tricky or demanding that we ignore or underrate the stuff that's good, lovely and beautiful. At times like these, I think it's really valuable to ask yourself: What am I grateful for? What do I appreciate in life right now? Just the act of writing these things down will help make sure that they stay in your mind.

Right this minute, I'm grateful for . . .

The chance to do something that excites and challenges me.

The knowledge that I'm surrounded by people who love and care for me.

Being healthy and fit enough to be able to exercise regularly.

Try to start keeping a list of the stuff in your life that you can be grateful for.

Everyone has myths they tell about themselves. Like all myths, they have a tiny grain of truth in them. They might be based on an experience we've had, or something somebody once said to us that stuck around in our brain. And, like all myths, the rest of them is pretty much made-up. BUT, because we carry on repeating them, this little grain of truth – wrapped up in a big bundle of make-believe – acquires a sort of reality. This reality is strong enough to affect the ways in which we think about ourselves. And the ways in which we think about ourselves impact on what we end up doing in our lives.

Maybe you once got on a skateboard and instantly fell off. That's the tiny grain of truth. What happens next, though, is that you draw a whole load of false conclusions based on the ten seconds it took for you to topple over. Instead of looking at it as a one-off accident or reminding yourself that learning any new skill is tricky and that you might not master it straight away, you convince yourself that you're NATURALLY bad at skateboarding. You tell yourself that you don't have the right sort of balance, or that your legs are too long/short.

So, although you'd actually love to skateboard yourself, you end up just watching your mates every time they go to the skatepark. Worse still, the longer this goes on, the more deeply that opinion of yourself gets entrenched. It might also spread to other parts of your existence. After all, myths are pretty potent! The fact that you've convinced yourself that you're rubbish at skateboarding could mean that you'll start thinking there's no point trying any other new things, because you'll probably be rubbish at them too. And why risk finding out? Why risk taking another knock to your confidence, which is already feeling pretty fragile at the moment, thank you very much?

It's so easy to get trapped in that way of thinking. It becomes an automatic response without you even noticing. You have that voice in your head that is always saying stuff like, *I'm so bad at this* or *I shouldn't have tried that.* Eventually it becomes impossible to see the world from any other perspective.

But you can actually start the process without ever once getting up off your bum.

Whenever you get stung by an unhelpful thought, try to challenge it with a helpful one.

THIS IS A PROCESS CALLED 'RE-FRAMING'.

Talking about ourselves in a negative way can become such an ingrained habit that we often don't notice we're doing it. It becomes as natural as breathing. But it's a habit that you can break with a little bit of effort.

Next time you find yourself saying something self-critical, try to say something positive about yourself to balance out the unhelpful thought.

Unhelpful thought: I fell off my skateboard, so I'm definitely, definitely, definitely the worst skateboarder ever, and should probably never even look at a skateboard ever again.

Helpful thought: I fell off my skateboard, but it's brilliant that I was brave enough to try something new. Next time I give it a go, I might do a bit better.

If you keep doing this, the moment will come when you'll find yourself doing it automatically.

WHAT WOULD YOU SAY TO A FRIEND AND WHAT WOULD THEY SAY TO *YOU?*

One way to break a cycle of unhelpful thinking is to try stepping out of your own head. If your mate told you that they were convinced they were the world's most rubbish skateboarder because they'd had one little crash, what would you say to them? Would you say the sorts of things to a friend that you would to yourself? If you wouldn't inflict those beliefs on somebody else, why the blimmin' heck would you do that to yourself?

Or (and you might need to be feeling a bit brave to do this one) why not share any unhelpful thoughts you have about yourself with a trusted friend or adult (there will be more about this in Chapter 5)? The strange thing is that, often, just by holding those thoughts up to the light, you realise they can be challenged or even overcome!

CHAPTER FOUR

WHY I'M NO LONGER SCARED OF MEETING NEW PEOPLE

A really important element of confidence is the way that you interact with other people. Having the world's best brain or being the world's fastest runner is great, but neither of these things means very much if you can't get along with other human beings. If you treat people kindly and with respect, if you make an effort to form connections with them by being curious about them, asking questions and really listening to the answers you get back, you'll reap amazing rewards. The energy that you put into the world generally tends to be the energy you get back from it!

Key qualities:
· Kindness
· Respect
· Curiosity
· Attentiveness

This is such a big subject that it definitely needs two chapters. In Chapter 5, I'll talk about why it's so important to have the right people in your life – and the impact that can have on your confidence. In this chapter, I want to discuss something that is also closely connected to everyone's confidence: meeting people.

Meeting new people can feel like an uncomfortable, intimidating process. It's the kind of thing that we tell ourselves we're rubbish at. In fact, it used to be the kind of thing that I told myself I was rubbish at.

There was a time in my life when nothing scared me more than the thought of walking into a room of people I didn't know. I'd get so nervous; I'd worry that nobody would like me, or that I'd have nothing interesting to say. I had these nightmares where I was surrounded by new people, all looking at me expectantly, and I'd open my mouth . . . and nothing would come out. After a while I got fed up of feeling like that. And I realised that I was avoiding doing things that I might enjoy, or that would improve my life, so I tried to change the way I approached these situations – because who wants to live a life that is narrowed and limited by your fear?

Now, you might already be familiar with a piece of advice that's often given to people who are nervous about standing up in front of an audience or walking into a room full of strangers. The thing that everybody says to do is to pretend that everybody sitting in front of you is naked. Once you've done that, the whole experience is less intimidating. Don't worry, I'm not going to suggest you do this (YUCK!) but I am going to propose that you change the way you approach meeting new people.

I decided that instead of seeing meeting new people as being like . . .

STEPPING INTO A SWAMP FULL OF SHARP-TOOTHED ALLIGATORS!

(AKA fixating on all the bad things that might happen), it would be far better to focus on all the good stuff that might come from walking into that room.

It's not impossible that you'll meet a new friend. Maybe even a new best friend! It's almost certain you'll meet somebody who you have something in common with, or who has had completely different experiences in their life that would be fascinating to hear about,

OR MAYBE IT'LL JUST BE SOMEONE WHO IS FUNNY AND MAKES YOU LAUGH.

And that's the attitude I take into every encounter with people I've not met before. I always think I'm going to encounter somebody who will improve my life in ways big or small. Maybe it will be something little like them telling me a good joke, or something more significant, like somebody offering me the chance to go on a cool adventure. But either way, this approach means that rather than being nervous about saying the wrong thing, or my trousers falling down – don't laugh, this once happened to a friend of mine – I'm actually excited!

Meeting people is the sort of scenario where the re-framing we talked about in Chapter 3 really comes in handy.

Let's say you're feeling nervous about having to go to a party where you won't know many people. It's possible that something like this – what psychologists call an 'automatic worry' – will be whizzing around and around in your brain . . .

'I'm so bad at meeting new people. I never know what to say. I'm either going to make myself look silly or hide in a corner until it's time to go home. Either way, it won't be fun'

The first thing I do in these situations is ask myself whether that automatic worry is realistic. Has it ever happened before?

In this example, I bet your automatic worry isn't realistic. You've been able to talk to new people in the past, and if your friend has invited you, that must mean that they like you! You must be doing something right!

So instead of listening to that automatic worry, why not try something like this . . .

'I've actually got some very good friends already, so I'm probably quite good at talking to people. I'll give it a go and see what happens. There might be a couple of awkward moments, but I bet I can handle them.'

Think of three or four different situations where you might meet new people. Maybe joining a club or going to a new school. Now try to list the good things that MIGHT happen when you go.

Another thing that really changed the way I approached meeting new people was realising it's not really that important whether *you* are saying interesting things. What's important is that you're interested in the person you're speaking to.

Being curious about another human being is a really great way of forming a connection with them.

WHEN YOU SHOW THAT YOU'RE INTERESTED IN SOMEBODY, YOU'RE SHOWING THAT YOU VALUE THEM AND WHAT THEY HAVE TO SAY.

That makes them feel good about themselves and encourages them to open up to you. It's also a great strategy to have up your sleeve when you're feeling anxious because you're worried that you won't have anything to say yourself. If you shift the focus to somebody else, you'll suddenly feel a lot less self-conscious. So, ask people questions, find out what they're interested in and what's important to them. You'll probably also discover the things you have in common. And if you have something in common, you'll find it so much easier to make that connection.

IT TAKES ALL SORTS
(AND THAT'S FINE)

Remember, there's no pressure on you in these situations. I reckon it's pretty likely that you'll hit it off with people when you meet them, because you're a fun, kind person. But if you don't, you don't! The fact that you haven't walked out of that room with a load of new mates isn't a reflection on you. It's not because you're too shy, or too talkative, or too serious or too silly. We're all really different – we can't be friends with every single person in the Universe.

Sooner or later we all find our own path, our own tribe. We all find the spot in life where we're comfortable. You will too. If somebody is going to be your friend, it's because they like you for who you are. So don't ever feel as if you need to fake anything, or be somebody you're not, just to make people like you. Don't force it or get worried. Remember, it's really stressful pretending to be a different sort of character to the person you really are.

I'm FASCINATED by other human beings; there's nothing I love more than trying to work them out. That means that I get really excited when I find myself surrounded by people who look at the world in a completely different way from me. Moving to France when I was a kid was a culture shock. Afghanistan, where I was posted in 2007 for the first time with the Royal Marines, blew my mind. I felt as if I was learning something new and amazing every day.

I was always keen to try to communicate with the people we met out there. Not long before we'd got on the plane to Afghanistan we'd been issued with crash-cards to help us learn a bit of Pashto, a language that a lot of Afghans speak. Quite often I'd get stuff wrong, and there were times when I just didn't know the word or phrase that the person I was trying to talk to was using. But you could always work out the general meaning by watching the speakers' faces. And, gradually, I got a bit more confident.

I remember one day when we had been sent on patrol to find out information about the movements of the Taliban, who were the opposing force. The Taliban constantly threatened the locals, and the villagers we encountered knew that if they talked to us they might be punished.

At some point, we reached a fairly big house, which stood on the edge of a small village. I walked over, my interpreter a couple of paces behind, and knocked on the door.

The head of the household, a man in his fifties opened the thick door a couple of centimetres and poked his head out.

When we asked him whether he could tell us anything about the Taliban's movements, he told us that he knew nothing. But I didn't believe him. His eyes wouldn't meet mine, and his knuckles were white where he was anxiously gripping the door.

As much as we tried, he kept refusing to say anything. Eventually he just slammed the door in my face. It was clear I'd need to try another way of persuading him.

I thought for a moment. Then, yes! I had it! We knocked on the door again and repeated how important it was that we could talk to him without being watched. While the interpreter was speaking, I mimed being able to smell something delicious, and said, *dodai*, the Pashto word for bread.

'Yes,' he said, still looking wary.

'Can we nip in, grab a bit of that delicious bread? Then we'll be on our way. We've been out on patrol for hours; we're all a bit hungry.'

This was something that I knew he could not refuse. One of the things about the Afghan villagers is that they're bound by a two-thousand-year-old tradition of hospitality called

Pashtunwali. If somebody, even if they're a stranger, comes to you asking for help, or food, or shelter, you have to offer it to them.

For a millisecond, he seemed surprised. Then he looked from me to the interpreter and back to me again, took a step back and beckoned my team in. I slung my weapon, took off my helmet and followed him into the courtyard of his home, where I bent down and played with his kids, talking to them gently. He returned with a huge piece of bread, and then handed it round: each of us breaking off a chunk before passing it on to the next man.

A few minutes of happy eating and playing with the children – who were all trying my helmet on and giggling – passed before we started talking again. By this time barriers had been broken down. We emphasised over and over again that we understood how afraid he was.

Next thing I knew he was bringing us tea (we ended up having TEN cups). As we were drinking it, he started holding my hand as we spoke – which I knew was a Pashtun sign of respect. 'Yes,' he told me, 'the night before last, a group of Taliban came through. I think they're still in the area.' Picking up enthusiasm, he told us everything he'd seen and heard. We came away with loads of valuable information.

What happened in that Afghan man's home was an example to me of the importance of being curious about other people. It was because I'd made the effort to learn about his culture that I'd hit on the idea of appealing to the tradition of hospitality. And it was because I showed him that I was interested in him and his problems that I was able to put him at his ease.

That desire to communicate made a big difference to my experience of being in such a different country. It meant I could form connections with other people – and connections are the building blocks of trust. The fact that I was willing to make that effort – and saw what difference it made – meant that I felt so much more confident walking into unfamiliar situations. It ended up making my life both easier and richer.

And what's true for a person in an Afghan village is also true for the mates you already have, and the mates you just haven't met yet.

BE CURIOUS ABOUT OTHER PEOPLE. GET OUTSIDE YOUR OWN HEAD. YOU MIGHT BE SURPRISED WHERE IT LEADS YOU!

People can be completely different from you. They might look at the world in ways you find unfamiliar, maybe even uncomfortable. But that doesn't mean you can't get along or find stuff that you have in common. In fact, I think that it's these differences that should be celebrated. After all, there is no such thing as 'normal'. The reason I'm so excited when I meet new people is because I know that whether they were born 500 metres away from me, or 5,000 kilometres, they'll show me new perspectives and different ways of approaching situations.

Write down three or four examples of times when you've met somebody who has taught you something new, or changed the way you think about a particular subject. This could be anything from a friend who has a different cultural background from you introducing you to a new dish (yummy!), to somebody challenging one of your preconceptions or prejudices.

Most of us are spending more time online, perhaps through Whatsapp calls, Minecraft or other online games connecting with people online as well as offline in the 'real' world.

These things have been a brilliant way for me to connect with people who I'd never normally get the chance to meet. I enjoy looking at what other people have been doing – the holidays they've taken, the new clothes they've bought, that selfie they took against a beautiful sunset.

But I'm always aware of how easily all these perfect pictures can lead to self-doubt, because you inevitably start comparing your life to theirs. It looks as if they're enjoying their BEST DAY EVER, over and over again. That might make you feel as if you're the only person struggling in a world where everybody else is smashing it.

However, it's just a filtered highlight reel that shows the fun, glamorous or enviable bits of their lives, while hiding all the tricky, upsetting or boring moments that fill the rest of their existence. Think how much difference all those clever filters can make to a selfie. Once upon a time only the super famous could edit the way they looked – now anybody with a smartphone can do it.

You might have seen this in your own life. You know that there's a gap between the smiling selfies your friend posts all day long and the problems they actually face. And the same is true of models, sportspeople, actors, musicians and TV stars (including me!). So whenever you feel that twinge of envy (and it will come from time to time), try to remind yourself of this. When you're looking at that person's 'perfect' photographs, ask yourself: What have they cropped out? What is missing from this picture?

This is also a good moment to remember that . . .

YOU ALREADY HAVE SO MANY REASONS TO BE CONFIDENT IN YOURSELF.

The people in your life who care for you will still love and look out for you whether you update your status every ten minutes or haven't actually even looked at your profile in so long that it's covered in dust and cobwebs.

Online communication can have a positive impact when we feel supported and connected. But this isn't always the case. Sometimes we use social media for no better reason than 'Everybody else does'. And so we don't stop to ask ourselves whether or not it makes us happy. Think about the following questions and see if the answers change the way you feel about online communication!

Do you feel better or worse after using social media?

When you feel down, do you feel as if using social media helps or harms you?

Can you imagine what a world without social media would look and feel like? Do you think you'd be happier and more confident?

> Whether or not you think that social media is having an impact on your mental health, why not consider taking a holiday from it to see what difference it makes to the way you feel? Set aside two days where you commit to not going online. See if you can persuade everybody else in your home to join you.
>
> After a break, do you feel more or less anxious?
>
> Does it change the way you see yourself and your body?

I always remind myself that my online personality is only a tiny part of what makes me special to others. Perhaps you can do the same?

EVEN A SMALL CHANGE IN PERSPECTIVE CAN MAKE A MASSIVE DIFFERENCE.

CHAPTER FIVE
FIND YOUR CONFIDENCE ALLIES

I'm obsessed with the jungle. I love its danger. I love its strangeness. I love the sheer, stupid SCALE of it. I love the fact that it's one of the last places in the whole world that you can take a few steps off the path you're on and think to yourself: No other human being has been here before. You get these flashes of what the prehistoric world must have been like before humankind arrived.

And I love the way it comes alive at night. If you lie in your hammock and switch your torch on, you can look down and see that the whole floor is moving. A sea of ants! But then you wake up the next morning, and they're gone, and you wonder: Was that all a dream?

That's why I was so excited when I found out we'd be doing an episode of *Escape* in the jungles of Papua New Guinea. *Escape* is one of the TV programmes I'm most proud of working on. Every episode was loosely inspired by a real-life disaster. Along with a team of other men and women, none of whom I'd met before, I'd have to try to build a vehicle from whatever we could find to hand that would help us get to safety.

In this one episode, we had to escape from the aftermath of a flash flood. All the other contestants were engineers, so their job was to do all the clever technical stuff. My job was to keep them alive!

Our campsite was miles away from the nearest village. We only had the clothes we were wearing and a limited supply of food. Oh, and we were surrounded by swamp, slime, the mysterious rustling of strange creatures in the undergrowth around us, and CROCODILES. We all worked with the mud creeping up our legs and sucking at our feet. We were constantly hungry, sweaty and every part of our bodies seemed to be covered by mosquito bites.

But the thing is, I loved that experience. Just as I've loved every other experience I've had of working as part of a team. It was brilliant seeing how every different person there had something to contribute. There was stuff I found challenging that others found easy. There was also stuff that they struggled with that I could help them with. We were all there supporting each other, doing what we could to work towards a shared goal. Everybody's voice was valued, and we all listened when somebody had a new idea. Working together, we were able to do something we'd never have been able to do alone. Gradually, we cobbled together a monster of a machine out of bits of broken-down motorbike and an abandoned bus. In the end, we couldn't get the boat to float, so in that sense we had failed the task. And yet it didn't feel like a failure to me. The real story, as far as I was concerned, was the way that everybody's confidence had grown over the days in the jungle. Being in a team had brought out the best in all of us. We all realised that other people can help us when we fall. Even better than that, they can make us stronger!

ONE IMPORTANT ELEMENT TO ACHIEVING TOTAL

CONFIDENCE

IS SURROUNDING YOURSELF WITH PEOPLE WHO ARE COMMITTED TO MAKING SURE YOU'RE AS

HAPPY & SUCCESSFUL

AS YOU CAN BE.

Very often, the things that look on the surface like individual achievements are only possible because of the contributions of a whole bunch of people. Think of Steve Jobs, the founder of Apple, the company behind the iPhone and iPad and a million other astounding pieces of technology. He was clearly a genius with a mega-brain. But none of that that would have been possible without the engineers and software developers he worked alongside. Serena and Venus Williams are extraordinary athletes blessed with extraordinary gifts, but they shared that success with a long chain of coaches (including their dad!), nutritionists, doctors and other types of support staff.

This is such an important thing to remember. Life is hard. Sometimes it can feel like an uphill struggle.

BUT YOU *DON'T* HAVE TO DO IT ALONE.

I couldn't do anything without the people that I love and trust by my side. People who believe in me and want the best for me. And I'm not alone. We all need that.

I'm confident not just because of what I know I'm capable of, **I'm confident because I know I'm supported by a network of people who love and care for me.**

Because I know that they're with me every step of the way, even tricky tasks feel more straightforward. Things that used to intimidate me, or that might once have felt so complex that my head started spinning, seem much less frightening. I even begin to look forward to them. When I'm around these people, I feel comfortable expressing who I am. I know I won't be judged when I fail, because I know they will still love and respect me, even if I make a mess of things. That makes me more willing to take risks and try new stuff.

I've got a small, close group of friends. They're not flash or famous. There's Mike, who is a businessperson and has become a kind of mentor to me. I've never met anyone busier than Mike, but he's always ready to listen to any problem I have. More than that, he's helped me understand that I'm capable of doing things that I'd always thought were beyond me. I can see that he believes in me and is cheering me on – that makes such a difference.

Arf and Jez are the Twinzz. They're so supportive and fun to be around. They accept me for who I am. They're really passionate about helping me build myself up to become the best version of myself that I can be. But they are also honest with me when I need to be told that I'm heading in the wrong direction.

And finally, there is Emilie, my wife. We're quite different in lots of ways, and yet at the same time we complement each other. Whatever has happened over the years (and a LOT has happened) she's always been there for me. I know that if I ever need to talk to her about anything, big or small, I can. She challenges, inspires and supports me. (She also makes AMAZING omelettes.) I'm so lucky to have her in my life.

ASKING FOR HELP

Whatever you're experiencing, it's always OK to ask others for help. That's what your friends and family are there for. Your happiness and well-being are really important to them – they want to be there for you. Maybe that will be by giving you advice when you're in a tough situation. Or perhaps they can help you look at that situation from another perspective.

The people who care for you could be friends, family, or even teachers. And each one of them will offer something different to you.

Perhaps they're the sort of person who makes you feel better about yourself whenever you meet up. Or maybe they're the kind of kid who, just before you're about to do something REALLY STUPID, taps you on the back and gives you the push you need to say 'No' and stand up for yourself. They could be people you sit back and relax with, or they can be people who challenge you and introduce you to cool new stuff. Sometimes they can do both.

These people will accept you for who you are. They don't want you to be different, they like you because you're YOU. They lift you up when you're feeling down. They build you up so that you feel strong enough to survive anything, which is all a long way of saying that . . .

OTHER PEOPLE CAN HELP YOU BE MORE CONFIDENT.

Spend a little time thinking of the impact that other people have on you. Think of a tricky situation you have experienced and how someone helped you through it.

What did they do that you valued? How did they help?

List qualities in your friends that have helped you feel more confident in yourself.

And, in return, why not do what you can to be the ally that your friends and loved ones deserve?

Being a supportive person to be around is such an important thing. I'll always try to be kind to everybody whose path crosses mine, no matter who they are. Because the nicer you are to people, the nicer they are back to you. Do people favours, pay them compliments, make them feel good about themselves. Remember to say please and thank you; open doors to other people; if you're having a sleepover at your friend's home, offer to clean up after dinner.

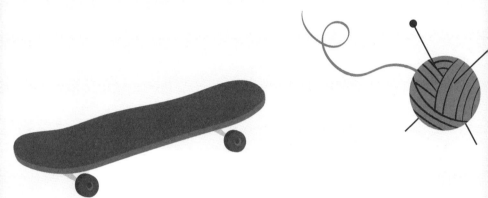

Whenever I meet somebody, whoever they are, no matter how old or young, I try to find out what it is that they care about most and then ask them questions about it. That could be anything from a cool toy to Ed Sheeran's music to rock climbing! I love the way that somebody's whole face comes alive when they're talking about something they love. The more you do this kind of thing, the more it'll become your natural reaction. You'll feel more at ease, and you'll help others feel comfortable around you too.

> **MISSION**
>
> *What can you do to make the lives of the people around you a bit better? It doesn't need to be a big gesture to make a difference. Maybe you could help your granny with her shopping? Or you could just remember to text your friend good luck before their big BMX competition?*
>
> *Try to think of at least three things you could do and give yourself a deadline by which you need to complete them.*

Being kind to others has an actual physiological effect on your body.

DID YOU KNOW THAT THE MORE YOU DO FOR OTHER PEOPLE, THE BETTER YOU WILL FEEL?

It's not just that it boosts your self-esteem (which means that your confidence grows and you're much more likely to try new things), it also floods your body with a lovely brain hormone (called oxytocin) that makes you feel both happier and healthier. Pretty cool, huh?

CHAPTER SIX
FOLLOW YOUR PASSIONS

Everyone has their own dreams, ambitions and passions. You might want to become an amazing dancer, or a novelist, or a famous actor ! Perhaps you just want to see if rugby is the sport for you or get deeper into the hobby you love.

All these things are different, but I believe that when you're doing things you enjoy, and getting better at them, your confidence soars. Scientific studies have shown that the happier you are, the more likely you are to see yourself and the world around you in a more positive light. You feel more motivated. Your sense of what you're capable of expands.

I feel lucky that I've been able to spend a lot of my life doing things that I'm passionate about. Sometimes that stuff comes to you by chance, but more often I've found that when it comes to discovering what you love, and then making the most of it, it can really help to have a plan.

I see plans as being a bit like a bridge. They're the thing that helps you get to places that used to feel out of reach. What I mean by that is that often the most interesting, rewarding things feel too distant or tricky to grasp. Because we can't achieve those dreams immediately, we convince ourselves that we NEVER will. But that's not how life works. Progress comes in little increments, not huge leaps. And plans help you make that progress.

BUT, and this is SUPER IMPORTANT, your happiness is more important than any single element of any single plan. So don't worry if you trip up or make mistakes along the way. And don't worry if at some point you decide that you want to change everything completely and start again.

Plans aren't an end in themselves. They're not the point of life. They're just a tool we can use to help us find our passions and achieve our wildest (and mildest) ambitions.

So, without any further ado, let me present to you . . .

When you're making plans, you need a What, a Why and a How.

WHAT

This is where you can be as creative or ambitious as you want. It's up to YOU! It could be that you just want to find a way of getting a bit better at basketball or singing because you really like doing them (which would be amazing and rewarding). But maybe you want to become an NBA legend, or a super-famous singing star. That would be brilliant too. What's important is that you should be the person who discovers how much you're capable of rather than letting somebody else decide it for you.

And remember that you don't need to become the best in the world at that thing. Just work out what success on your own terms might mean.

Consider the sort of person you'd like to be. You might find that drawing that person helps you visualise them. What would they look like? What would they be doing? What sorts of relationships do they have? What types of activities do they like? What kind of home do they live in? Just imagine it; it doesn't have to be realistic, but I've found that drawing that person you might want to be in the future helps show you what your values are, what you appreciate and what makes you feel happy right now.

WHY

A boxer friend of mine once said that 'There's no point in climbing into the ring and taking punches if you don't know why you're doing it.'

You need to have a good reason why you're doing what you're doing, because that's what will keep you going when things get a bit wobbly, or you get stressed out. That's why it's so important that your ambitions and dreams should be things you have chosen for yourself. They've got to be something you want, not a path you're following because you want to please other people, or because you think it's expected of you. When you know why you're getting out of bed early to go to swimming practice or scraping your knee after you've fallen off your BMX yet again while trying to perfect a new trick, it will be far easier to keep going on those days when your energy or enthusiasm dips. You'll be able to take setbacks in your stride, and you'll be less likely to give up.

So find something that excites you; that grabs hold of you and won't let go. Because the more you enjoy something, the more you'll want to work hard at it. There might come a point when it doesn't even feel like work! And the more you put into something, the more you'll get out of it.

HOW

One of the most important elements of any plan you draw up – whether that's your practice schedule for a flute exam, or your goal of becoming the first person to walk on Mars – is breaking the task before you up into manageable chunks. Otherwise you'll just feel overwhelmed.

If you're going to take up the guitar, don't tell yourself that you want to be shredding awesome solos within a week. Just focus on a series of small, achievable targets that will eventually add up to the moment when you walk on stage in a puff of dry ice and the crowd goes WILD (or will just make sure that you're a little bit better in six months' time than you are now).

Maybe you want to find somebody who will teach you the basics first. Work out how to play a few chords, then once you feel comfortable doing that, go to the next stage. There's no rush! The happier you are with the route you take, the more you'll try and the easier you'll find it to keep going when you hit a bump in the road.

One last thing. Do you know what separates the best athletes, musicians, artists and designers from everybody else? Do you know what helped me become an elite soldier?

HARD WORK.

THE WILLINGNESS TO PRACTISE OVER AND OVER AGAIN.

THE WILLINGNESS TO KEEP TRYING EVEN WHEN THINGS GET TOUGH.

If you want to make your dreams become a reality, at some point you're going to have to roll up your sleeves and WORK! But, eventually, it pays off. The more you work, the more you practise, the more confident you feel.

IT'S NOT JUST YOU!

You're not the only person who sometimes struggles. I know how easy it is to feel disheartened when you look around and it seems as if everybody else is brilliant at everything. The thing is: this isn't true! While we all have our own individual strengths, we also have our own individual weaknesses. That kid who aces every single biology test might be rubbish at music. And what's probably also true is that the biology whizz works REALLY HARD, you just haven't noticed it.

HOW TO KEEP GOING WHEN YOU'RE TEMPTED TO GIVE UP

Sometimes your motivation will dip because you feel tired, or pressed for time, or you've had a couple of setbacks. Or it might be that some of the stuff you need to do to reach the fun, exciting goal is actually a bit dull and complex. Endless practice is probably the best way to massively improve your basketball shot, but it can probably become boring. VERY BORING.

And so, although you really want to do it, you end up procrastinating instead. Or you tell yourself that you're too busy to do it. You can't magic motivation out of the sky.
And that's where discipline comes in.

I'm not talking about soldiers shouting in your face (which isn't good for anybody's motivation). Being angry with yourself because you're low on enthusiasm isn't going to help you. It'll just end up making you feel worse! What I mean is creating a space in which motivation can grow again.

I remember that I once talked to a woman who was desperate to get fit. She really wanted to do it! But life kept getting in the way. She was always too busy to go out for a run. Something always came up when she was thinking about going to the gym. The only advice I gave her was to commit to getting up half an hour earlier three times a week, and then using that time to exercise.

That's what she did. And she stuck with it. First, she started to feel a little bit fitter (not much, she'd only just started). Then there was a psychological change. The fact that she'd proved to herself that she could keep to her new schedule made her feel really good about herself.

She realised that she was capable of more than she'd imagined even a month ago. Proving to herself that she could stick to that routine filled her with confidence. And from that point on her motivation started FLOWING!

You can do exactly the same. Don't ask too much of yourself, and don't set yourself unrealistic targets. If you get over-excited and say that you're going to devote ten hours every day to learning how to speak Spanish, you're guaranteeing that you're going to fail. But if, twice a week, you need to get up earlier to work on your piano scales, or sacrifice half an hour of watching TV every Thursday so that you can fit in going to football practice, then that's what you're going to have to do. I never said this would be easy, did I??? And yet I promise you it will be worthwhile. Showing yourself that you're able to maintain that discipline, even when sometimes you're feeling tired or bored, will help boost your confidence AND your motivation.

We can't change our habits overnight. It takes time! So we need to be willing to persevere.

Whatever it is you'd like to do, no matter how big or small, you'll really struggle to make progress if you can't find the time to do it regularly, for a sustained period of time.

If you want to introduce a new habit into your life, psychologists recommend devoting ten minutes every day (or at least five times a week) to a new habit for a period of at least four weeks.

If you've already got a dream or ambition, how about spending ten minutes or so thinking about how you could find the time to devote your energy to it on a regular basis – forming a new habit! Do you have to give up doing something else to fit it in? Or can you just rearrange your schedule a bit?

This is also a good opportunity to practise your 'I' statements, because it's likely you'll need to communicate your needs to somebody like a parent, or teacher or friend. So, for instance, you might want to say something like: 'I want to go for a run five times a week. It makes me feel good and I will prioritise this in my life.'

I believe that you are capable of achieving so much. I also know that not every plan works out. There will be times when no matter how much work you put in, no matter how carefully you prepare, you'll fall a bit short. You shouldn't worry about this at all. I'll never tire of saying this, but failure is a part of life. Everybody's journey through life has its own shares of blips. Nobody will ever succeed at everything and we all have our days that feel difficult.

A failure doesn't mean you're worth any less. It doesn't mean you're no good. It just means that you've had a setback. SO DON'T GIVE UP. And don't let it affect your confidence. **BE KIND TO YOURSELF.** You're still the same awesome person, whatever has happened.

It's really good to do a bit of self-reflection after you've had a setback. If you can, try to identify *why* you weren't able to reach your target. Not so that you can beat yourself up about it, but because learning something from the experience helps you grow.

Now, I can see that you might think that the very last thing you'd want to do while those wounds are still raw is revisit them. But owning our failures, and taking lessons from them, is a good way of helping build our confidence.

When we do this, we're demonstrating that we can survive any setback, and that we can, in fact, emerge stronger.

Make a leap back in your memory and think of a few occasions when you felt as if you failed at something. Maybe you were put in the lowest maths set at school and felt it was unfair. Or maybe you didn't stand up for a friend who was being teased.

Once you've done this, ask yourself, how would I approach the situation next time? What did I learn about myself?

When you've had a setback, it's also really important to avoid telling myths about yourself. (See page 56 for more about this.) If you give yourself too much time to stew in your failure, you're much more likely to slip into this way of thinking about yourself. So, once you've spent a bit of time reflecting on the experience, try to throw yourself into a new project before too long. This could be simply re-attacking the same problem or finding a new one. Get out there and prove to yourself and everyone around you how brilliant you really are.

CHAPTER SEVEN

FEEL THE FEAR AND GO AHEAD ANYWAY

The world is full of brilliant, exciting things. Some of them we're aware of already, and others are mysterious and unexpected. Taking big (or small) leaps into new spaces, opening yourself up to new experiences and challenges, can be intimidating. The idea of trying something for the first time can be frightening. I often feel that same sense of nervousness when I'm on the brink of stepping into the unknown. I get a chill down my spine and a sort of jangly feeling in my tummy.

But I don't let that anxiety stop me, because I know that it's also a sign to me that I'm doing something new and exciting. It's a sign that I'm opening myself up to new opportunities. I'm giving myself a chance to grow.

One day in 2015 I got a call out of the blue from a man who said that he was a TV producer. He explained the concept and asked if I had any interest in coming in for an audition. At that point I was trying to build a security business in Africa. The idea of going on television didn't figure in my plans. It wasn't that I thought it was an impossible goal; it was literally inconceivable. When I was in the Specialist Military Unit I couldn't tell anybody, not even my family, what I was doing or where I was going, and now somebody was asking me if I wanted to go on national television!

I had no idea whether I'd be any good onscreen (I'd never done anything remotely similar before) and I had no idea whether the show would be a big hit or a disastrous failure. I knew nothing about how television programmes were made – it was an entire Universe that was almost completely alien to me.

But I could feel a little buzz of excitement. *This is something new, unlike anything I've ever done before. Why don't I give it a try? And what if it works out? What if it ends up being really fun? What if I have an amazing experience irrespective of whether it succeeds or fails?* So I said, 'Brilliant, sounds good. When do you want me to come in?'

The whole experience of being on television, and everything that has followed, has been incredible for me. Truly life changing. And yet if I'd focussed on all the things that could have gone wrong, I'd have told the producer I wasn't interested. And you wouldn't be reading this book right now!

THE POWER OF JAZZ!

I'm not the world's biggest fan of jazz (if you're not sure what jazz is, imagine musicians playing music that they improvise – they may start off going 'doodle-doodle-doodle' and then suddenly out of nowhere start going 'skronk, whizzzzzzz, SKRONK, WAAARGH').

However, you don't need to like jazz to learn from it. The people who play it really value spontaneity. They don't stick to the same notes every time, they improvise: if a note feels right, they play it! You might very well ask: 'Ant, what's this got to do with me?'

And my answer would be that as important as it is to have plans, it's equally important that you give yourself the space to adapt or even abandon them when circumstances change. None of us can see into the future. We can't predict what exciting opportunities and challenges life is going to put into our paths. And we don't even know how we ourselves are going to evolve over time. At the age of ten, you might be obsessed with the Solar System. Two years later, your chief interest might be street dance! I spent a huge period of my life devoted to the military, and yet now I'm interested in so many other things. I've become a different person. I have really different priorities.

If, when the TV producer had called, I'd insisted that I wanted to pursue my long-term plan of building a security business, I'd never have given myself the chance to explore a completely new kind of life and career.

So don't be too rigid in making or keeping your plans. Always be ready to embrace the brilliant things out there that you *haven't* anticipated or planned for.

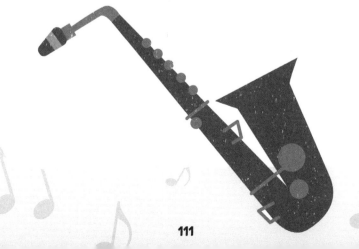

Do you remember me talking in Chapter 2 about how embarrassing it was the first time I tried to speak French to a class full of French kids? Well, there's a sequel to that story.

In the days after the incident, I got fixated on saying everything perfectly. I was obsessed with getting the pronunciation correct, and I wouldn't even open my mouth unless I was sure I was going to say exactly the right thing. And, of course, that meant I never said anything.

My brother had his own way of doing things. We'd started out knowing pretty much the same amount of French, but he took a completely different approach from me. He'd just start talking and see where it took him. He made loads of mistakes, and lots of his conversations ended up being a mix of English, French and funny gestures, but he always seemed to manage to get his point across. And the strange thing was that the more he did this, the better he got.

When he got something wrong (which he did a lot) he smiled and carried on. He didn't mind when a French child or teacher pointed out where he'd gone wrong. And he almost never made the same error twice.

THE FACT THAT HE WAS WILLING

TO GIVE IT A GO

WITHOUT BEING
WORRIED ABOUT STUFFING
EVERYTHING UP WAS LIKE A

SUPERPOWER.

HIS ATTITUDE WAS:
WHAT'S THE

WORST THAT COULD HAPPEN?

And he was abso-flipping-right. For him, the advantages he knew he'd gain by learning French and being able to start making friends with the local kids completely outweighed the possibility of making a few errors, or maybe feeling a little silly to begin with.

Ever since, I've tried to take the same approach. That's what I did when I got that call from the TV producer. I know that there's always a possibility that when I try something new it won't go well. But I'm OK with that. If I do trip up, I can just pick myself up, learn whatever lessons I need to, and move on. Because **what, really, is the worst that could happen?** You join a theatre club and find you don't really like acting after all. SO WHAT? You play in a tennis tournament but don't get beyond the first round. WHO CARES?

Can you think of a time when you were really worried about trying something new, but everything actually worked out fine and you ended up having a brilliant time? What are the things you like doing now that you wouldn't have in your life if you hadn't been willing to take that little risk and give them a go?

Find a bit of paper and write them down. Maybe it was joining that theatre club, or maybe it was that time on holiday when you overcame your nerves about meeting new people and started chatting to the kid your own age who was staying in the same hotel as you?

MISSION

The other thing that I've learned is that the 'perfect opportunity' doesn't exist. It's a legend, like unicorns or the Loch Ness Monster or pots of gold at the end of the rainbow. The truth is that everything you ever try will always have the potential to go a bit wrong. Or it will contain some element that's a tiny bit less than ideal. The danger comes when you spend your life passing up really cool opportunities because you're waiting for that one 'perfect' opening.

To me, the worst thing that could happen would be missing out on an exciting adventure, or the chance to meet somebody brilliant, because I've focussed on the worst things that could happen, not the best. Or because I've dismissed that opportunity because it's not completely perfect. Think how many times you've not wanted to go to a party because you feel a bit nervous about new places and new people, and then you get there and have an INCREDIBLE time.

Don't get hung up on getting stuff wrong – throw yourself into new situations and experiences. You'll soon find yourself reaping the rewards! Every time you do this, your confidence will grow (win or lose). And the more confident in yourself you start to feel, the more likely you are to grab the exciting opportunities that come your way. Which will in turn make you even more . . .

CONFIDENT.

I know how easy it is to get obsessed by all the things that could go wrong. As well as spending time contemplating the advantages, another thing you can do when you're considering learning a new skill, or going on a new adventure, is to take a few moments to contemplate what sorts of problems you might encounter. So far, so normal. But here's the twist.

Take a moment to consider the situation you find tricky.

What are your worries around it?

It is good to feel prepared and have a plan for these situations. Although there are often times when we can't control what is happening, we can think about ways to respond that help us feel calmer.

List some actions you could try if things don't go to plan when facing something new.

Maybe you could chat to a friend about it and hear their views.

Or you could take some time on your own to walk, relax and do an activity that you enjoy.

You could write a journal to express your feelings in words. This can help you think more clearly about something, and sometimes the act of writing things down brings great ideas!

This might surprise you, but one of the things that a lot of soldiers are most afraid of (even more than bullets and fighter planes and everything else on the battlefield) is looking silly in front of their mates.

What's saddest is that this fear of being laughed at actually ends up holding a lot of us back. The thing that other ex-soldiers say to me more than anything else is that they wish they'd tried out for the Specialist Military Unit. 'Well, why *didn't* you?' I always ask them, even though I'm 90 per cent sure I know the answer already.

What they tell me is always a variation of the same thing: they couldn't bear the idea of having to come back to their mates and tell them that they'd failed. They were convinced that they'd be laughed at.

The thing is, in one respect, they are sort of right. I remember when I told the other Royal Marines in my unit that I was considering going on Selection, which is the super-tough series of tests you need to pass in order to become a Specialist Military Unit soldier. A few of them tried to put me off, warning me that I'd fail – because the overwhelming majority of candidates do – and end up making a fool of myself. A handful even laughed at me right there and then. 'You'll never make it, so why put yourself through all that pain?'

I know that doing this sort of thing – where you're putting yourself out there – can feel overwhelming, even frightening. But where they were wrong, REALLY WRONG, was letting that fear of being mocked stop them from doing something they'd dreamed about. Sometimes you do need to be brave and ignore those fears. I used to see it as a bit of necessary pain, like when you have to rip a plaster off. The older I get, though, the less I feel the need to be brave. That's not because people are any less likely to point and laugh at me; it's because I've realised something: why should I care what they think?

One of the big things that stops us from trying new stuff is a fear that it'll be too hard. It's so easy to shy away from learning a new skill or trying a new activity. So easy that after a while it becomes an automatic reaction. We end up never doing anything new or challenging. It becomes another one of those myths I mentioned earlier. We tell ourselves that if something is hard, we won't be able to do it. And yet hard isn't the same as impossible.

We all find loads of things difficult. That's just a sign that you're stretching yourself. And if you're stretching yourself, you're learning and growing. We forget that we probably found a lot of the things we now enjoy and take for granted really tricky and intimidating to begin with.

We also forget that, actually,

THE PROCESS OF WORKING SOMETHING OUT THAT SEEMS CHALLENGING CAN BE INCREDIBLY REWARDING.

Think how satisfying it is to finally master a tricky skill. You can feel your neurons firing, leaving you feeling exhilarated.

If you have a bike, you probably put hours into practising how to ride it. You'll have struggled to co-ordinate your balance and whizzing the pedals around. You'll have made a bit of progress then wobbled all over the place before falling off and grazing your knee. You'll have looked up at whoever was teaching you and said: 'I CAN'T DO IT! IT'S TOO HARD!'

And then, one day, all that effort paid off and everything came together. You sped off at top speed, hearing yells of, 'COME BAAAAAAACK!'

You probably don't give it a second thought now.

If something is hard work, that usually means it's worth persisting with. The achievements we value most, the achievements we are most proud of, are almost always those we worked hardest for.

Change your relationship with difficulty. Instead of finding ways to evade it, why not seek it out? *Think of three ways you could challenge yourself.*

For example, if you find confrontation intimidating and usually shy away from it, perhaps you could look for an opportunity to stand up for yourself, or others. Maybe your mates are at your house but nobody is letting your little brother have his go on the games console, even though it's clear he's feeling sad. Perhaps, instead of watching and looking forward to your turn, you can speak up and make sure your brother gets to play too (even if it feels embarrassing and difficult)?

If you're normally right-footed, why not try to use your left foot next time you're at football practice? You'll probably feel frustrated to begin with, but why not carry on for one more drill? And then one more. And then one more . . . After all, what's the worst that could happen?

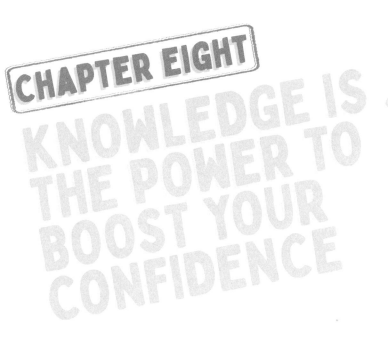

CHAPTER EIGHT

KNOWLEDGE IS . . . THE POWER TO BOOST YOUR CONFIDENCE

I'm going to be honest with you. I didn't have the best time at school. I was too much of a fidget, my attention span was always too short. I messed about and chatted far more than I should have. Which meant that I ended up leaving without any qualifications.

I thought education and learning was something you did because you had to. I saw it as something that was expected of you by teachers and parents and a lot of other old, boring people. I just wanted to be left to my own devices – I didn't see the point of ANY of it.

It was being in the military that transformed my relationship with learning. Even when I was a raw recruit, I knew that I wanted to get to the very top and join the Specialist Military Unit. The thing was, I had no idea what I needed to do to get there. There was a very simple answer: become one of the best soldiers in the whole Armed Forces! Which, of course, isn't *quite* as straightforward as that. You could make yourself a better soldier by working really hard – going out on extra runs, turning up for extra target practice. And I did all that. But the thing I realised would set me apart from everybody else was learning as much as I possibly could.

That's when I became really hungry for knowledge. I understood, then, that the more I knew, the further I'd be able to travel. I signed up for every course I could, I badgered older, more experienced soldiers until they shared all of the stuff that they'd learned with me. I pushed myself, doing everything I could to accumulate more information, more skills.

That's why, when we did target practice, I started to carry a little notebook around with me, and recorded everything I did. Every time I went onto the shooting range (and I did that a heck of a lot), I'd measure then scribble down the wind strength, the humidity, the barometric pressure and the air pressure, before noting what adjustments I needed to make to hit the target. I did the same thing in every kind of environment and condition until making those adjustments – whether that was to the way I breathed or accounting for the rotation of the Earth – became automatic to me.

I put everything into that learning because I could see what a difference that knowledge was making to my career. At school I'd viewed education as an annoying chore I had to get out of the way before I could start to live my life properly. But I had been SO WRONG. I completely missed the point. Education and learning aren't something you do for other people. It's not even really about qualifications and exams, it's something you do FOR YOURSELF.

When you learn new things – whether that's how to calculate the circumference of a circle or mastering a tricky move on FIFA – you're giving yourself the chance to grow.

YOU'RE ADDING AWESOME NEW TOOLS TO YOUR ARMOURY. YOU'RE BECOMING MORE CONFIDENT.

LEARNING IS WHAT HELPS YOU

ACHIEVE YOUR

DREAMS.

And it's also what helps you adapt to new situations –
being hungry to learn new things was what helped me make
a success of going on TV. I found that the more I learned,
the more confident I became.

As someone once told me, 'You're never going to get anywhere worth going if you don't learn the things that are worth knowing.' BUT I've also learned enough to know that I don't know it all. Far from it. And that's nothing to be ashamed of. In fact, I reckon it's a good thing.

When I started working in television, I knew absolutely nothing about what actually went into making a show. Each day when we went out on set, I'd feel overwhelmed and confused. Invariably I'd end up standing in the wrong place, or talking to the wrong camera, or sometimes both. Occasionally somebody would ask me something that they thought was really basic, and I'd just look at them blankly, as if they were squawking instead of talking.

I realised I could do two things. I could pretend that I actually knew what was going on. Or I could admit what everyone already knew: I was completely new to this and needed help. 'How do I do this?' 'What's that called?' 'When should I start talking?'

The thing is, THERE'S NO SUCH THING AS A SILLY QUESTION. Even when I was putting my hand up and looking quizzical for probably the millionth time that day, the camera operators and directors and runners were all patient with me. They could see that I was trying, that I was willing to learn. My experience is that people want to help you. Nobody expects you to know everything –

especially when you're still a kid! They'd much prefer to be bombarded by a million queries about how to do something than for you to pretend you are a world expert in the subject, and then make a mess of it because you've got no flipping clue how to do it. **It's the sign of being a confident person when you're happy to admit you don't know something**. It's OK to ask questions! How else would you find out?

I know that I'm not the finished article now and I'm never going to be. That's cool with me. Who the flip would ever want to reach a point where they no longer had space in their life to grow, improve and change? And it's actually dangerous to persuade yourself that you know everything you need to – because that's when you close your eyes and get complacent. And when you close your eyes and get complacent, you stop learning, you stop growing.

That's why I'm not afraid of what I don't know. I'm EXCITED by it. It's brilliant knowing that there are new skills and facts and tricks waiting for me to discover them.

What's absolutely crucial is that you find a way of learning that works for you. One of the things that I found tough when I was a kid, and still really gets me now, is the idea that there's a RIGHT WAY and a WRONG WAY to learn. Joining the military showed me that **there are so many different ways to learn.**

THE GREEN-EYED MONSTER

We all get jealous sometimes. We see somebody grab first prize in the singing contest that we'd thought we had a chance in. Or win a part in the school play that we desperately wanted. Or maybe they just appear to be better at getting along with others than we are.

That jealousy gnaws away at us inside. We end up having thoughts that we know aren't nice, and the more we have them, the worse we feel. We can't even think about that other person's achievements without making unfair comparisons to ourselves.

But there are always going to be people who are better than us at stuff, whether we're playing sports, computer games or the piano. We don't gain anything from feeling threatened or resentful. Instead of competing with others, why not try to look at them for inspiration? How did they do so well? What can we learn from them? What can we do differently?

If you're really into reading, then books (*especially* this one) probably will be one of the best ways for you to learn. But you might be the sort of person who prefers watching films or talking to other people who can share their wisdom with you. Or it might be that what really helps you is a combination of all three. Or none of them because you have your own method. Everybody is different!

WHAT REALLY HELPS ME LEARN IS TO ACTUALLY DO THE THING IN QUESTION.

So if I want to learn how to roller-skate, I'll read the books and watch the video tutorials until I'm sick of them. And yet I don't feel I'm making progress until I actually put my skates on and start rolling around. I'll probably end up getting things wrong and falling onto my bottom – there will be a certain amount of trial and error – but it's only by getting my hands dirty (metaphorically) that I can really begin to understand the process.

Do you know what helps you to learn? Spend a few minutes thinking about those times when you've felt really excited as you learned new information. What was it about the way that you absorbed that information that you liked? Why do you think you responded so well to it?

I've listed a few different methods of learning here. On another piece of paper, write down what you like and don't like about them.

*   *Reading books*

*   *Listening to a teacher*

*   *Watching a video*

*   *Trying something for yourself*

Now that you've finished, has your opinion about what way of learning suits you best changed?

MAKE FEEDBACK YOUR FRIEND

If you've read *Mission: Total Resilience*,
you'll know that I think it's SO important
to embrace feedback. But I also know that
even the most constructive, well-intentioned
feedback can feel as if it's taken a chunk out
of your confidence. Say, for example, you've
put everything you could into a school project.
Anything, no matter how small, the teacher
says is going to hurt. You want to shout:
'DON'T YOU KNOW HOW HARD I WORKED?'

You need to remind yourself that they're not
calling your project rubbish or writing you
off. The fact that you've got a couple of sums
wrong doesn't mean you're a terrible person.
They've given you those comments BECAUSE
THEY BELIEVE IN YOU and want you to become
the best version of yourself that you can be. So
don't let feedback undermine your confidence.
If you listen to that feedback, then learn from
it, you'll do even better next time round. And
guess what? You'll become more confident as
a result. HURRAH!

I have always tried to find out as much as possible about my surroundings and the people in it. You could do the same intelligence gathering when it comes to turning criticism from something that hurts into something that helps! If you seek out feedback yourself, it's easier to embrace it.

Who do you know who could offer you feedback? Make a list of three people, and then ask them to be honest with you.

Here are some examples to give you inspiration:

You would like to know how to draw people's faces so they look more realistic – maybe you could ask the art teacher?

You hurt your friend by saying something careless. You've made up now, but could you talk to them about how to avoid offending them in the future?

CHAPTER NINE
YOU CAN DO IT!

I want you to know that I believe with every atom in my body that anything I can do, you can do too. So let me tell you a story from my time in the military ...

I hadn't been in uniform for very long when I was summoned into the presence of a warrant officer to discuss a letter they'd received about me. To begin with, I felt pretty happy with the way the meeting was going. The letter praised me for the work I'd done as an interpreter for a French officer. It turns out that my time in Normandy had really come in handy! But that happiness didn't last for long.

'Why not go down that route?' the warrant officer asked. 'Why don't you train as an interpreter? Your French is an amazing skill to have. You're fluent and

I don't understand why you haven't tried to take advantage of it before now. There's so much you can do with it.'

But that just wasn't the path I wanted to follow. I loved being a soldier; I was desperate to travel, to experience more, and perhaps one day join the Specialist Military Unit. I didn't want to spend my life helping French officers have EXTREMELY TECHNICAL conversations with their British equivalents (unless you like conversations about vertically-integrated vector logistics, in which case you would have found them EXTREMELY INTERESTING.)

When I told the warrant office that I was flattered, but the life of an interpreter wasn't for me, he suddenly became a bit less positive.

'Look, Middleton, I'm trying to do you a favour here. I'm not going to insult you by hiding behind pretty words. You're too small. That's a fact. You've done well to get this far, but ultimately your physique's going to be a liability. It's a real shame. But there it is. There's a six-month interpreter's course in Beaconsfield. You'd come out with a qualification. And, between you and me, it'd be a nice, easy spell. Think about it. No need to rush your decision.'

WHAT????? This felt devastating to me. I thought I'd been doing well, but he saw things completely differently.

I went back to my room with my head fizzing with self-doubt. And then I realised something. When I'd gone into the warrant officer's room I'd been convinced that I had what it took to be a really good soldier. The fact that he had offered his opinion didn't really change anything. What I turned to in that moment was my self-belief.

I HAD ALREADY ACCEPTED WHO I WAS, AND WHO I WASN'T. I KNEW THAT THERE WERE THINGS I LOVED DOING AND WAS GOOD AT. I ALSO KNEW THAT I WASN'T PERFECT.

I was never going to be a big giant of a recruit. I was always going to make mistakes – because everyone does! I couldn't change that. And yet, realising this wasn't the same as saying that I was just going to give up. I'd had a few struggles before. But I'd always made it through! I'd showed everybody what I was capable of. I was passionate about my plans and willing to work hard. I was keen to learn and had the support of people who I knew loved and cared for me. And I knew that even if I did trip up along the way, I'd be able to pick myself up and try again.

So I didn't go on that interpreter's course. Over the years that followed, I tried and tried and never stopped believing in myself. It wasn't an easy or straightforward route. I went off course a few times. And there were times when I was tempted to give up. But slowly, steadily, I made my way forward. I joined the Royal Marines, then finally got into the Specialist Military Unit. And that, in turn, opened the door to so many exciting, brilliant things for me after I left the military.

I'm telling you this story because I was only nineteen then. I had the same self-doubts you probably do. I was still growing into my body and my mind (actually, I reckon I'm *still* growing in my body and my mind!) but I was also passionate about the dreams I had – just as I bet you are.

What's exciting is that over the next few years of your life, you're going to change and grow in all sorts of ways.
I know that you're already an incredible, kind, funny human being. I hope that this book has helped you to see that.
I also hope that it's something you can turn to whenever you need a boost, or on those tricky-feeling days when the world seems like it's against you.

CHAPTER TEN

THE TEN STEPS TO TOTAL CONFIDENCE

1. YOU'VE ALREADY GOT SO MUCH TO BE CONFIDENT ABOUT

Appreciate and accept the person you are right now. You're not perfect (nobody is!) but you've already been smashing it for years. Think of everything you've achieved, everything you're capable of, every tricky situation you've survived, and all the people that love and care for you.

2. IT'S POSSIBLE TO BUILD CONFIDENCE, STEP BY STEP

If you can prove to yourself what you're capable of by slowly, patiently learning new skills, you'll feel ready to face anything.

3. YOU MIGHT NOT BE ABLE TO AVOID DIFFICULT SITUATIONS . . .

. . . but it is possible to change the way you respond to them.

4. SOMETIMES WE ALL HAVE AN UNHELPFUL VOICE NARRATING OUR LIVES . . .

. . . but you can change that into a helpful voice.

5. MEETING NEW PEOPLE DOESN'T NEED TO BE A SOURCE OF ANXIETY!

Cultivate your curiosity, search for common ground and focus on all the brilliant things that will follow when you encounter people who see the world in a different way from you.

6. WHEN YOU HAVE A SUPPORTIVE NETWORK OF PEOPLE AROUND YOU, YOUR CONFIDENCE WILL SOAR!

Other human beings can provide the supportive foundation we need to help our confidence grow. Why not try to do the same for them?

7. PLANS ARE BRILLIANT FOR HELPING YOU GET TO WHERE YOU WANT TO GO

But they're just tools. Don't let them trap you. Always leave yourself free to change or re-define both your dreams and ambitions, and the route you want to take to reach them.

8. DON'T LET YOUR FEAR OF WHAT MIGHT POSSIBLY HAPPEN NARROW OR LIMIT YOUR LIFE

Take risks, be open to new opportunities, be prepared to make mistakes – because, really, what's the worst that could happen?

9. BE EXCITED ABOUT ALL OF THE THINGS YOU DON'T KNOW YET

The more you learn, the more confident you'll feel. But never forget that a wise person knows enough to know how little they really know!

10. CELEBRATE OTHER PEOPLE'S SUCCESSES, SUPPORT THEM WHEN THEY FALL . . .

. . . but remember that whether they're bigger or smaller than you, whether they're better than you at speaking German, or worse than you at climbing trees is COMPLETELY IRRELEVANT. The only thing that matters is that you feel happy and fulfilled.

I don't expect you to remember this all at once. There might be some steps that you want to come back to later. Don't worry.

If you take anything at all away from this book, it should be this:

GO OUT THERE.

BE *BRAVE*. TAKE *RISKS*.

TRY NEW THINGS.

OPEN YOURSELF UP TO THE WORLD, BECAUSE THERE'S SO MUCH FOR YOU TO EXPLORE, SO MUCH FOR YOU TO LEARN **and** EXPERIENCE.

YOU CAN DO IT!

THE MISSIONS

You can read *Mission: Total Confidence* in whatever order you want. And there might be some chapters you want to return to when you're facing a specific challenge or task. To remind you of the key lessons from each chapter, I've collected all the missions that appear throughout the book together in one place. You can work through them whenever and however suits you. And remember that even if you manage to finish only one, you're still making progress!

MISSION 1 (PAGE 19)

Take a moment to consider all of the difficult stuff you've managed to cope with already. Write a list of things you have found challenging but have overcome and things you are good at. Perhaps you made a new friend on a school trip that you'd been nervous about going on. Or maybe you love drawing and can create pictures that make you feel happy.

MISSION 2 (PAGE 20)

I believe that doing *something* is always better than doing *nothing*. When you're actively trying to provide solutions to problems, it helps you feel more in control of that situation and gives your brain less time and space to get all twisted up with uncomfortable thoughts. That's true when it comes to those one-off events in life that make you anxious (like the prospect of having to go to a new school), but it's also true when it comes to the stuff that feels quite challenging in your everyday life (maybe you find meeting new people hard).

It's also important to remember that 'doing' doesn't have to involve jumping around and being super active. It could just be sitting still for a few seconds and trying to notice what thoughts are swirling round and round in your brain. Don't hide from those feelings or pretend that they're not there. When I can sense anxiety mounting inside me, I turn to face it. 'Oh hello, feeling of worry, why are you here? Can you leave now please, I do not need you!'

Write down three things you love and enjoy doing, and three challenges you're currently facing. Now, beside each one, write what you can do to make the most of those things you love, or what you can do to overcome those challenges. For example:

Something I love: I'm good at badminton.
If I practise more I might be picked for the team.

Something I feel challenged by: I hate the idea of
standing up and speaking in front of large groups.
If I try to give some little presentations to smaller
groups first, I'll gain confidence.

MISSION 3 (PAGE 22)

Draw a picture of yourself on a
piece of paper and then add some
thought bubbles with positive
things about yourself (use the
list you created in the mission on
page 19 to help you).
For example:

I am loved.
I am brave.
I make people laugh.

Hang it up on your wall and try saying one of
the positive statements every day to help you
remember why you're special.

MISSION 4 (PAGE 37)

Make a list of five new things you'd like to try. Next, write down what first commitment you could make to begin. It can be really small, but remember, every step forward counts!

So, for instance, you might be interested in helping to fight climate change and have discovered that local activists hold meetings in a venue close to your house. BUT, the idea of standing up and sharing your thoughts and ideas in front of loads of people sends a chill down your spine. Your first commitment could be going to one meeting. Next time, maybe you could put your hand up and ask a question. These are all tiny steps. Tiny commitments. But they add up. And who knows where this will lead you?

MISSION 5 (PAGE 45)

Why not give these power poses a go? They'll send a load of confident messages to your brain. They'll also communicate that confidence to anyone you interact with.

1. Keep your chin and head up (a tip for helping with this is to imagine that your top of your head is connected by a string to the ceiling).

2. Stand up straight (put your shoulders back).

3. Stand with your feet in a wide, open stance.

4. Keep your hands out of your pockets.

5. When you're talking to somebody else, smile and maintain eye contact (if this is something you find difficult, you can try to look at the other person's eyes for two seconds, then their nose for two seconds and then their mouth for two seconds – then repeat. This gives the same effect as looking directly into their eyes.)

MISSION 6 (PAGE 49)

Start to use more 'I' statements in your everyday life. Perhaps you could begin by practising in front of a mirror?

Then you can build up to sharing those opinions with close friends and family. Once you feel comfortable doing that, why not start putting your hand up more in class? What does it feel like to share your opinions and feelings in this way? Does it make you feel confident? Does it change the ways in which other people respond to you?

You could also consider using your voice to help others. If you're in the playground and you see a group of kids being mean to someone, then why not speak up? You could confront the bully yourself, or if you'd prefer, tell an adult. Be a superhero in your own school!

MISSION 7 (PAGE 55)

All of us are far too quick to forget, or take for granted, the good things in our life. This isn't surprising. We can often be so busy focussing on the stuff that feels tricky or demanding that we ignore or underrate the stuff that's good, lovely and beautiful. At times like these, I think it's really valuable to ask yourself: What am I grateful for? What do I appreciate in life right now? Just the act of writing these things down will help make sure that they stay in your mind.

Right this minute, I'm grateful for . . .

The chance to do something that excites and challenges me.

The knowledge that I'm surrounded by people who love and care for me.

Being healthy and fit enough to be able to exercise regularly.

Try to start keeping a list of the stuff in your life that you can be grateful for

MISSION 8 (PAGE 58)

Talking about ourselves in a negative way can become such an ingrained habit that we often don't notice we're doing it. It becomes as natural as breathing. But it's a habit that you can break with a little bit of effort.

Next time you find yourself saying something self-critical, try to say something positive about yourself to balance out the unhelpful thought.

Unhelpful thought: I fell off my skateboard, so I'm definitely, definitely, definitely the worst skateboarder ever, and should probably never even look at a skateboard ever again.

Helpful thought: I fell off my skateboard, but it's brilliant that I was brave enough to try something new. Next time I give it a go, I might do a bit better.

If you keep doing this, the moment will come when you'll find yourself doing it automatically.

MISSION 9 (PAGE 65)

Meeting people is the sort of scenario where the re-framing we talked about in Chapter 3 really comes in handy.

Let's say you're feeling nervous about having to go to a party where you won't know many people. It's possible that something like this – what psychologists call an 'automatic worry' – will be whizzing around and around in your brain . . .

'I'm so bad at meeting new people. I never know what to say. I'm either going to make myself look silly or hide in a corner until it's time to go home. Either way, it won't be fun'

The first thing I do in these situations is ask myself whether that automatic worry is realistic. Has it ever happened before?

In this example, I bet your automatic worry isn't realistic. You've been able to talk to new people in the past, and if your friend has invited you, that must mean that they like you! You must be doing something right!

So instead of listening to that automatic worry, why not try something like this . . .

'I've actually got some very good friends already, so I'm probably quite good at talking to people. I'll give it a go and see what happens. There might be a couple of awkward moments, but I bet I can handle them.'

Think of three or four different situations where you might meet new people. Maybe joining a club or going to a new school. Now try to list the good things that MIGHT happen when you go.

MISSION 10 (PAGE 73)

People can be completely different from you. They might look at the world in ways you find unfamiliar, maybe even uncomfortable. But that doesn't mean you can't get along or find stuff that you have in common. In fact, I think that it's these differences that should be celebrated. After all, there is no such thing as 'normal'. The reason I'm so excited when I meet new people is because I know that whether they were born 500 metres away from me, or 5,000 kilometres, they'll show me new perspectives and different ways of approaching situations.

Write down three or four examples of times when you've met somebody who has taught you something new, or changed the way you think about a particular subject. This could be anything from a friend who has a different cultural background from you introducing you to a new dish (yummy!), to somebody challenging one of your preconceptions or prejudices.

MISSION 11 (PAGE 76)

Online communication can have a positive impact when we feel supported and connected. But this isn't always the case. Sometimes we use social media for no better reason than 'Everybody else does'. And so we don't stop to ask ourselves whether or not it makes us happy. Think about the following questions and see if the answers change the way you feel about online communication!

Do you feel better or worse after using social media?

When you feel down, do you feel as if using social media helps or harms you?

Can you imagine what a world without social media would look and feel like? Do you think you'd be happier and more confident?

Whether or not you think that social media is having an impact on your mental health, why not consider taking a holiday from it to see what difference it makes to the way you feel? Set aside two days where you commit to not going online. See if you can persuade everybody else in your home to join you.

After a break, do you feel more or less anxious?

Does it change the way you see yourself and your body?

MISSION 12 (PAGE 87)

Spend a little time thinking of the impact that other people have on you. Think of a tricky situation you have experienced and how someone helped you through it.

What did they do that you valued? How did they help?

List qualities in your friends that have helped you feel more confident in yourself.

MISSION 13 (PAGE 89)

What can you do to make the lives of the people around you a bit better? It doesn't need to be a big gesture to make a difference. Maybe you could help your granny with her shopping?

Or you could just remember to text your friend good luck before their big BMX competition?

Try to think of at least three things you could do and give
yourself a deadline by which you need to complete them.

MISSION 14 (PAGE 94)

Consider the sort of person you'd like to be.. You might find
that drawing that person helps you visualise them. What
would they look like? What would they be doing? What sorts
of relationships do they have? What types of activities do
they like? What kind of home do they live in? Just imagine it;
it doesn't have to be realistic, but I've found that drawing
that person you might want to be in the future helps show
you what your values are, what you appreciate and what
makes you feel happy right now.

MISSION 15 (PAGE 102)

We can't change our habits overnight. It takes time! So we
need to be willing to persevere.

Whatever it is you'd like to do, no matter how big or small,
you'll really struggle to make progress if you can't find the

time to do it regularly, for a sustained period of time.

If you want to introduce a new habit into your life, psychologists recommend devoting ten minutes every day (or at least five times a week) to a new habit for a period of at least four weeks.

If you've already got a dream or ambition, how about spending ten minutes or so thinking about how you could find the time to devote your energy to it on a regular basis – forming a new habit! Do you have to give up doing something else to fit it in? Or can you just rearrange your schedule a bit?

This is also a good opportunity to practise your 'I' statements, because it's likely you'll need to communicate your needs to somebody like a parent, or teacher or friend. So, for instance, you might want to say something like: 'I want to go for a run five times a week. It makes me feel good and I will prioritise this in my life.'

MISSION 16 (PAGE 104)

It's really good to do a bit of self-reflection after you've had a setback. If you can, try to identify *why* you weren't able to reach your target. Not so that you can beat yourself up about it, but because learning something from the experience helps you grow.

Now, I can see that you might think that the very last thing you'd want to do while those wounds are still raw is revisit them. But owning our failures, and taking lessons from them, is a good way of helping build our confidence.

When we do this, we're demonstrating that we can survive any setback, and that we can, in fact, emerge stronger.

Make a leap back in your memory and think of a few occasions when you felt as if you failed at something. Maybe you were put in the lowest maths set at school and felt it was unfair. Or maybe you didn't stand up for a friend who was being teased.

Once you've done this, ask yourself, how would I approach the situation next time? What did I learn about myself?

MISSION 17 (PAGE 114)

Can you think of a time when you were really worried about trying something new, but everything actually worked out fine and you ended up having a brilliant time? What are the things you like doing now that you wouldn't have in your life if you hadn't been willing to take that little risk and give them a go?

Find a bit of paper and write them down. Maybe it was joining that theatre club, or maybe it was that time on holiday when you overcame your nerves about meeting new people and started chatting to the kid your own age who was staying in the same hotel as you?

MISSION 18 (PAGE 116)

I know how easy it is to get obsessed by all the things that could go wrong. As well as spending time contemplating the advantages, another thing you can do when you're considering learning a new skill, or going on a new adventure, is to take a few moments to contemplate what sorts of problems you might encounter. So far, so normal. But here's the twist.

Take a moment to consider the situation you find tricky.

What are your worries around it?

It is good to feel prepared and have a plan for these situations. Although there are often times when we can't control what is happening, we can think about ways to respond that help us feel calmer.

List some actions you could try if things don't go to plan when facing something new.

Maybe you could chat to a friend about it and hear their views.

Or you could take some time on your own to walk, relax and do an activity that you enjoy.

You could write a journal to express your feelings in words. This can help you think more clearly about something, and sometimes the act of writing things down brings great ideas!

MISSION 19 (PAGE 121)

Change your relationship with difficulty. Instead of finding ways to evade it, why not seek it out? *Think of three ways you could challenge yourself.*

For example, if you find confrontation intimidating and usually shy away from it, perhaps you could look for an opportunity to stand up for yourself, or others. Maybe your mates are at your house but nobody is letting your little brother have his go on the games console, even though it's clear he's feeling sad. Perhaps, instead of watching and looking forward to your turn, you can speak up and make sure your brother gets to play too (even if it feels embarrassing and difficult)?

If you're normally right-footed, why not try to use your left foot next time you're at football practice? You'll probably feel frustrated to begin with, but why not carry on for one more drill? And then one more. And then one more . . . After all, what's the worst that could happen?

MISSION 20 (PAGE 131)

Do you know what helps you to learn? Spend a few minutes thinking about those times when you've felt really excited as you learned new information. What was it about the way that you absorbed that information that you liked? Why do you think you responded so well to it?

I've listed a few different methods of learning here. On another piece of paper, write down what you like and don't like about them.

• *Reading books*

• *Listening to a teacher*

• *Watching a video*

• *Trying something for yourself*

Now that you've finished, has your opinion about what way of learning suits you best changed?

MISSION 21 (PAGE 133)

I have always tried to find out as much as possible about my surroundings and the people in it. You could do the same intelligence gathering when it comes to turning criticism from something that hurts into something that helps! If you seek out feedback yourself, it's easier to embrace it.

Who do you know who could offer you feedback? Make a list of three people, and then ask them to be honest with you.

Here are some examples to give you inspiration:

You would like to know how to draw people's faces so they look more realistic – maybe you could ask the art teacher?

You hurt your friend by saying something careless. You've made up now, but could you talk to them about how to avoid offending them in the future?

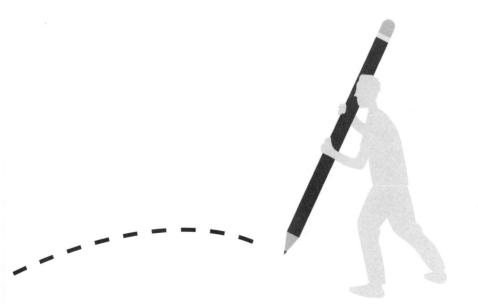

ARE YOU READY FOR TOUGH TASKS AND FUN CHALLENGES?

Your mission, if you choose to accept it,
is to learn how to become super resilient.

I challenge **YOU** to maximise your potential,
supercharge your self-esteem, unlock your inner
strength and turn setbacks into opportunities.

YOU'RE STRONGER THAN YOU THINK!

ANT MIDDLETON is an adventurer, public speaker and television presenter. He is the author of six *Sunday Times* bestsellers, *First Man In*, *The Fear Bubble*, *Zero Negativity*, *Mental Fitness*, *Cold Justice* and *The Wall*. His books have sold over two million copies around the world. When he's not climbing Mt Everest, or jumping out of helicopters, he likes to spend time with his wife and children.

Consultant **DR MIQUELA WALSH**, DEdPsych, MsC (Dist), BSc (Hons), HCPC accredited, is an Educational Psychologist who supports children and young people with a range of emotional, social, and learning needs.